About the Author

Tango Yankee wants to thank you for picking up this book; you have helped her achieve one of her most ambitious dreams, and she hopes the same for you.
Dear reader, the world has its arms open for you, and she hopes you embrace it and never let go.

Pretty, Pretty

Tango Yankee

Pretty, Pretty

Olympia Publishers
London

www.olympiapublishers.com
OLYMPIA PAPERBACK EDITION

Copyright © Tango Yankee 2024

The right of Tango Yankee to be identified as author of
this work has been asserted in accordance with sections 77 and 78 of the
Copyright, Designs and Patents Act 1988.

All Rights Reserved

No reproduction, copy or transmission of this publication
may be made without written permission.
No paragraph of this publication may be reproduced,
copied or transmitted save with the written permission of the publisher, or in
accordance with the provisions
of the Copyright Act 1956 (as amended).

Any person who commits any unauthorised act in relation to
this publication may be liable to criminal
prosecution and civil claims for damage.

A CIP catalogue record for this title is
available from the British Library.

ISBN: 978-1-80439-692-6

This is a work of fiction.
Names, characters, places and incidents originate from the writer's imagination.
Any resemblance to actual persons, living or dead, is purely coincidental.

First Published in 2024

Olympia Publishers
Tallis House
2 Tallis Street
London
EC4Y 0AB

Printed in Great Britain

Dedication

I dedicate this book to my best friends and my family, who are one and the same. I don't know how I got so lucky to have you; you are my whole world and more.

Acknowledgements

Thank you to Olympia Publishers for believing in this book; you have given me something priceless, and I am eternally grateful for your support and belief in my most adventurous dream.

Dear Reader

I want to fall in love with you
Dear reader

I want to crumble in your arms
And feel your chest lift with breath

I want us to play and lay
In the folds of these pages

I want your clothes frumpled as you sleep
Amongst these enjambered characters

I want you to watch me love you
Languorously to sleep

We can show each other such delicate worlds
I cannot wait, dear reader

POEMS ABOUT INVISIBLE THINGS

I wrote these poems in hopes of giving words to some of the whirlwind emotions a person is feeling, in hopes of them gaining clarity to their struggle. These poems were points of healing for me, and I hope that reading these poems could be a small step in the healing process for somebody else and provide another perspective on trauma, grief, mental health struggles, criticism, paranoia, fear and loss. Throughout reading these poems: breathe. Breathe power. Know that there is always love in the corner of every dark room.

Yellow Walls

Sharp words puncture your sweet sentences
As a baby-cousin is sent stumbling away
The door closes with numb quietness
And something toxic fills the room

A girl, confused and out-of-place
Thinks she is wrong to feel the violation
And still instinct tells her to shake her head
While her privacy is popped like a balloon

It's a game she doesn't like playing
She knows something is wrong
But the look in his eyes and the urgent certainty of his hands
makes her statue

And she is in no pain, but the harsh bright lights on yellow walls
And the bewildered, sullen young face in the mirror for the days to come
As she sees a child who is very good at keeping secrets
Especially when she felt threat before she knew what the word emotion meant

Years later, her stomach rings at the memory
She reads and re-reads her ticket to a court-case win
The letter he wrote that calls her "precious"
The letter she wrote back calls him "psychopath"

She shoves chairs into glass windows

And shatters mirrors on the ground
She is so lonely and so she tells everyone
Boring them with the noxiousness of it

She won't visit the country to which he escaped
But she will try find his face in old family photos
She will say she is healed
When she fears strangers with square-rimmed glasses and crooked smiles

She is not dramatic despite what she tells herself
She is still confused and out-of-place
Blocked by a memory she no longer flinches at
Healed in a straitjacket

Except this type of healing looks shattered and violent
This type of healing dismantles an innocent love story
This type of healing crumbles her at the door of intimacy
She doesn't know what healed is
But it feels like she needs to punch something with her broken fists: the yellow wall in front of her face until the bricks yell mercy
And cry on the other side with a pride that nobody else understands

They say "you're not alone," but she needs to fight this by herself
They say "you can't let him win," but they aren't in the ring
They say "be strong," but they don't know what strength is

Because strength was eighteen months of silence
From the age of four to five
But by then maybe she had already healed
Incorrectly
With scar tissue around her heart

And all we have left is a patient who runs away
From open heart surgery for
You cannot cut out the scars
If now they form part of the walls

She is scared
Confused and out-of-place
And people don't understand a lot about her,
One being

In her own way, she has won

Fiddle

If I were an instrument, I would want to be a piano
But you made me a fiddle because you wanted to be a fiddler

A Spoilt Brat Moment

My room is a fucking mess

I haven't unpacked my moving-in boxes and it's been weeks
I have some crinkled clothes in the washing machine
But I don't know how to make the fucking washing machine work and I don't have the "right" powder and
Even if I did I don't know what buttons to press and then I will just have a whole lot of wet clothes (still stained) and nowhere to hang them

My cupboard is a fucking mess

There is tupperware everywhere
Open biscuits packets and crumbs and dead ants
Exotic tea that I never drink and even if I did it wouldn't matter 'coz I put so much sugar in it how could I taste the rhubarb and? Whatever else is in it
The vitamin B tablets I should be taking that make my room smell like an expired chemist
The those choc chip cookies because fuck knows when I want them I need them

My wallet is a fucking mess

Slips that I don't know whether to keep or throw away
It's either the corner of a condom packet or of the seasoning you put on popcorn but who gives a fuck
And the money I have I wanted to spend on my parents or my brother or my boyfriend but... I also want a blender so

I'll be incentivised to eat breakfast

But I need money to drive places even though I don't have a license or a car, and I can't go through the stress of "Oh fuck I can't buy this donut because then I can't get back to my dorm"
And then I'll uber home and cry coz I can't eat a fucking donut

I am… just a mess.

And the Disorder Eats Her

She hates eating food because she loves being skinny

But she loves eating food because she is always so hungry

And she hates being skinny because she always feels so sick

But she just really loves being skinny…

Well
That is if she ever gets skinny

22:48 – 27th January 2022

I had an existential crisis today
It seems I am having those quite often now
Every time I'm alone in a room
And every time it gets a little worse

Little things give me comfort nowadays
It seems that everyone and everything has an expiring date
And the things that do give me comfort
Tease me with wakefulness when I am under anaesthetic

Because all I have to look forward to is the next time
I feel this small pocket of heavenly comfort
Which seems to be so far away most of the time
And all I feel in between is desperate

I'm addicted to these blissful moments
That seem to never come
And the insecurity seeps in that
Time doesn't stop for comfort

Time passes like a flood
Time is good at drowning me these days
In a river my own mind wept

I am a servant to it, a player in a video game
I'll just sit here and experience my circumstances
Because I guess that is the point of life
If you aren't forced to struggle with daily physical survival

And all those algorithms for happiness are fraudulent
No numbers stand the test of a million tons of water moving at impossible speeds
Water drowns mathematics too
That's exactly why floods collapse buildings
Submerge roads
Break houses from foundations
Floods cause the ultimate act of surrender

Humans are so advanced that we are our own destruction
We are the things that cause the most of our pain
Our thoughts are the rain of the flood

And so it won't get better when I am alone
It'll get worse
That is why I need to talk to somebody
That's why I want to talk to somebody

I need to talk to some body

00:30 – 24th March 2022 – I Don't Like Her

I don't like the way she leaves food on the counter
And how packed her fridge is
I don't like that she will throw away the canned soup
She opened the day before because it smells funny
Even though it is still good food
I don't like how her clothes are everywhere collecting creases
I don't like the way she is too lazy to pick them up

I don't like the way she cries for attention
Victimises herself even though her life is amazing
I don't like the way she eats loudly and talks while chewing
And she doesn't brush her teeth, so she always smells bitter

I don't like the way she burrows herself a hole, lies there in self pity
Expects other people to fall at her feet and dig her out
I don't like the way peer pressure is her favourite drug

I don't like the way she is always looking in the mirror
'Coz I really don't like the way she looks in the mirror

And she is such a hypocrite
I don't like the way she doesn't drink water
She doesn't care about obvious things
I don't like the way she doesn't read books any more
How she has abandoned the things that she loves

I don't like her selfishness

I don't like her jealousy
I don't like her damsel-in-distress act
I don't like how she is always thinking of herself
Yet how she has given up on herself too

I don't like being alone with her
I don't like so many things about her
And I hate the way she criticizes herself

16:52 – 30th April 2022 – Exoskeleton

Dear Dear

I've forgotten who you fell in love with
I lost her quite some time ago
And I'm broken because you're somehow still in love?

Don't Let Love Spoil

The fridge is full of rotting food
The half-eaten packet of spinach is wilting
The milk has curdled a long time ago
The forgotten yoghurt is surely nuclear by now
The bread has even let you down
The avo is only good enough for mush and
The cucumber has frozen resiliently to the freeze tray
The bananas are oozing this sticky brown sap
And the mangoes are bruised, brown and brethelling in the deep darkness under your cold soggy pizza box

You have too much
Nowhere to put it all
No way to use it all

But you have too much instead of too little
It's the same with love
It's abundant
Unconditional
Engulfing
Stupidly stubborn
And loud
Too much, not too little

All you have to do is open the fridge
Don't let love spoil

Veins

Black blood runs through my veins
Burnt-smelling oil spilt in the ocean
Beating through inflamed blood vessels like tides

It swells my heart
And slows my limbs
It blinds the synapses of my mind

Loose fluids runs out my eyes
Slides through my fingers, burning them
Bleeds onto my clothes

The sting grips me by the throat
Making me cold inside out
It's like my bone marrow hurts

I need leeches and lobotomies
A straight jacket for this new dark thing
Dialysis for my brain

A doctor stumbles into the asylum, sage angel
She draws a curtain into my brain
Shocked by the mould inside…

She pulls out a long metal stand
With a hooked bag of golden liquid

I tell her that the blackness needs to be drained first
But she taught me one thing that I'll never forget: blood always regenerates

The Unspoken Signs of a Victim

She snaps
She grabs
She pulls
She breathes
She screams
She hits
She looks
She guides
She moves
She moans
She weeps
She slips
She sucks
She bites
She blinks
She runs
She weeps
She shrieks
She wakes...
She breaks

Surgery

Sometimes rape can be gentle
Like smooth warm hands

Sometimes a rapist can be friendly
Like soft smiling eyes

Sometimes violation can be tentative
Like stepping into a cold cold ocean

But the knife still rips the same
No matter the topography of its edge

The anaesthetic still doesn't exist
Only the wound

The Roses Were Blue

Love was the bitter taste of roses after the fifteenth fight
Love was years sleeping apart because divorce is laborious
Love was buying new cars with shopping bags full of silence
Love was obligation

What you are experiencing is a little girl who
Thinks love is a moving satellite when it is in fact the sun

Treat her gently because she is scared of it
The sting of water on a new sheet of skin that grew
Like tissue paper over the third-degree burn

She only knows the brokenness
Teach her.

Granny, What Happened to Him…

He had such a fickle relationship with the past
His eyes used to stare blankly at the screen and now they brim at the seams when he watches the birds in the trees
The newspaper was used as the heart of the fire and now he clings to them like relics
The words on his lips are of the fruits trees in the garden no more news and politics

Granny, what happened to Grandad?
He used to be so strong
He used to walk like he wasn't skating on ice
He loves the fudge I make even though he is diabetic…
Granny, what happened to Grandad?

"Nothing, my love, just a… mid-life crisis."

17:41 – 5th August 2022

There was a time in my life where everything beautiful made me think of what my last day would look like

There was a time in my life when I almost ruined everything

Until I realised self-destruction was destroying so much more than just the empty feeling in the pit of my stomach

Allergic

I wish thoughts were food
So I could vomit up the rot

Amphoteric

You take drugs, and I am forgiving
You need support, and I run
You are stubborn, and I always yield
You don't care because I do
You have the right to drag me through the mud because I am too clean

At what point do I draw the line and say that you don't love me, you love the power you have over me?

Drinking to Chase Sobriety

My mind has too much control over my body
It winds itself around who I am
And constricts the authenticity
I don't drink enough
Because when I drink
I don't think about how my face looks when I smile
I have friends and not social colleagues
The world is an experience rather than a struggle

Time is pulled towards me
The weight is off my back
I don't drink enough
Because the thoughts already have me drunk
And they have me drinking alone

- Disclaimer: drinking did not help

Being a Terrible Human

You broke something in me
But broken things break whole things so easily
Smashed vehicles are so much sharper than functional ones
So I am starting to question if it even was your fault
For what you did to me was so fundamentally incorrect but what I did to you was unforgivable

Br-Ache Up

The heaviness
The ache
It's my own garden rocks
It's the wood you axed down
It's every word I said to hurt you
It's every word that you ignored
It's the mass
Of a ton of feathers
That just won't blow away in the wind
It's the unforgiving weight
Of death
When the one you grieve is still breathing
They just do not want you in their life anymore

Sad-Byes

Your kisses will fall like autumn leaves
Your goodbyes will be heart-breaking
When we kiss we cascade the seas
If only it weren't my head shaking

Watching you leave, buying your ticket
My heart in your hands and crying
It is hard to take you seriously I will admit it
When you say you'll never stop trying

I want your hands on my neck, the gaze of a fool
Your eyes speaking melodies to convince me
Call me selfish and call me cruel
But, please, please don't leave me

Thief

Give me back my heartbeat

I know you stole her
Like you did
That one stop sign
That one night
In the fizzy silence
When you felt like
Being reckless
And now you have
A novelty
To show your friends

I will walk into
You room and seize
The photo you keep of us
Because you were
Too lazy to take it
Down or your ego
Kept your self-righteousness
So well contained

And I will take her back,
My little heartbeat
From the box you keep
All your memoirs
I will rescue her
Because you don't even
Have the respect
To give her back
Yourself

Sky

We looked at the same cloud
You saw a sunset
I saw the storm
The difference was that you had the sun on your side
And I was alone
And when we both smiled at the sky
You tried to embrace me, but I pulled away
Because our strengths are not the same
And I have diluted myself for so long already
It is time for me to have colour again

Horticulture

Someone leaves
A hole, a hollow
And you panic like you will never have a beautiful garden again
But someone leaves
A hole, a space to breathe
A space to let fallow, my friend

But someone leaves
A hole, a little pocket
For little weeds, unbeknownst to the florist
And this is what cracks:
You gasp, grip with such contrite because nothing will grow where once bloomed a stunning plant

The weeds came out in fists of rage and you stuff it with dry rocky soil and went on pretending it didn't exist

Like there wasn't a piece of your smile that died and fell off your face the day he left

It is okay to water your garden with salt today

It is an art, an underrated skill, to fill a hole with the seeds a plant has left you when the plant is no longer there to fill the hole itself

The Pen in Your Hands

Heal long term or heal short term
You choose what addictions you're allowed depending on the answer

And Your Soul Lives On

You are no longer on this Earth
You are part of the ground
You feed the trees who feed us
And so in your death you give
Others life and I wonder if the
Higher Power knew that they
Granted everybody the most
Selfless gift in death, how you
Chose to live your every day

POEMS THAT ARE PRETTY TRUE

The Honest Hypochondriac

Sometimes I think there is something wrong with me
because I want something to be wrong with me

The doctors with sincere tones will tell me it's severe
Faces will fall when I tell my loved ones the news
I would use it as an excuse to stay home
For my pale complexion
My rapid weight loss

Sometimes I think I am a sadist
Because I think about my funeral

I think about what will be said at my funeral
I wonder about the stories that would be told
How the injustice ripped through my family
How they all wished to talk and hug me, but I was no longer there

People who didn't care would suddenly care
Sweating with cold guilt about all the things they said to hurt me
All the friends that were never friends
All the teachers that never noticed me would now cherish me
They would reread my poems and call me an artist, a genius, Van Gogh

And they would say all the nice things that I wish they'd say when I was alive

I would feel the love with pumping blood

Sometimes I think I am sick enough
To wish I was sick enough to nearly die

I would imagine the faces of the nurses
How they would cry after I am knocked unconscious

Because I am so scared that I will never wake up
And they are too

How the paramedics dial in my phone to phone my emergency contacts
How their hearts would fall when they would see my wallpaper
A photo of my sweet golden retriever

How my family will sleep dreamlessly next to the hospital bed
How they would ask the nurses to improve their menu for me
Talk to me like I was about to go on stage to perform a monologue

Is it a crime to want to be critically cared for? If only for a moment?
Sometimes I wish I was as hurt physically
As I have been emotionally

Because then the people around me will treat me like I'm hurting
Which sometimes I really am

Blueberry Muffin

I could take the car for a lonesome road trip; I could take myself out for takeaways and play obnoxiously loud music in the parking lot. I could cry without anybody hearing; I could disappear and leave all my books scattered on my bed. I could leave the half eaten blueberry muffin exactly where it is; I could drive out to the top of the hill to see the lights and watch the cars on the highway. I could drive to the house of somebody I know, and we could sneak out and shoplift a few chocolates from a petrol station. I could go to the richest street in North Cliff and ring the doorbells of the fanciest houses and run away like an idiot. I could hop the fence to my school's rugby field and run the whole length in the dead of night. I could go to my old house and see how the new interior designer has polluted the play room with floral pillows and marble vases. I could go to a bar and help the workers stack up chairs after a long night; I could visit my cousin and tell her to not ever do what I am doing but I'll smile while I say it. I could dance in the middle of the road; I could do donuts at empty intersections. I could be anywhere doing anything right now.

But I am not.
I am sitting in my room, it's raining and I can't sleep
And all I am doing is wondering (fruitlessly) about all the things I can do… but am not.

I Feel Cold

The days you walk with your thoughts and not your feet,
The weather does not make you feel anything in particular
Everything feels grey and on the edge of falling

Yet, you're only thinking about someone you love

Their fingers aren't pressed against your closed lips but you feel silenced
Their body isn't on yours but your chest still feels the pressure
You feel scrutinised but their eyes haven't fallen on you in a long time

When you are uneasy with this dank feeling
Insecurities seeping through your clothes, into your hair,
You soak in it when you fall asleep
When you look into the eyes of strangers they see it and when you look into the mirror you see it yourself
The water you drink is laced with this chronic heaviness because you love them more
Than they love you

It's called compulsive obsessive love disorder
And it is to do with nothing of love
But rather the absence of it

01:00 – June 5th 2022 – The Truth

I stood bundled in your arms
In our own little world
I looked deeply into your eyes
And for a second wished you read my mind
"I need you to need me."

"I need you…"
You pulled me in closer
As you lied to me for the first time.

I, a Book

I sit on the shelf and watch you stumble about
Crying and laughing through your hardships
Admiring the artwork you rambunct across the room
Feeling the warmth of the fire you build yourself

It's just such a pity that I, the book, once a stoic storyteller,
have become merely more than paper leather-bound
Cursed but with no intentions of looking out of the window
Contentedly waiting for you to open me
Dismissive of dust on my cheeks

I sit here holding the words to our story
Solemnly so close to my heart
The fields we dance through
The abandoned buildings we explore
The moon that guides our bare feet
We get lost in the waves of the oceans
And out footfalls fall silent in the forest
And suddenly the pages run dry
And the words slip over the edge
Onto the floor

The floor I refuse to look at
When I can be staring at you

I, a book, waiting for you, an author, to complete our story
A story that has become one of neglect

A Critic's Hand Guide to Self-Care

I mean this with only love
Be better
Think
Work harder
It's not good enough
Your decisions
Your behaviour
You disappoint me
Frustrate me
You're a hypocrite
Self-righteous
Immature
And careless
Grow up

Me? What about me?
How dare you judge me?
Tell me I'm not enough
How dare you expect perfection?
Diligence
Selflessness from me
Just cut me some slack
I'm allowed to have flaws
Be human
I don't deserve this
I've been through enough already

There's a sparkle in your eye
Tears?

Emotional manipulation?
You think that's going to work?

Come on
Be real
Be better

You inanimate object
You cheap piece of glass

The Day after My Driver's License

What I bought...

Disposable camera
Cherry sweets
Zam bak
A goldfish
Snacks
A peanut butter syrup iced coffee
Sunglasses

A little bit of freedom

Hurt

Hurt is a loan
It grows over time
If you don't throw something at it
Every now and then
Give it a real punch
It can slowly surround you
And take away important things in your life

Ageing

Ageing must be one of the scariest things
Not because of the porous bones
The atrophied muscles
The wiring of my thick silky hair
The blurring of the eyes

But the memory loss...

My biggest fear is forgetting my greatest memories
Losing the faces of the kindest strangers

When a cemetery becomes just a garden of oddly-shaped flowers

Losing things that will never exist if I don't find them

An every-day drug trip
So mild I don't even realise it is happening

It terrifies me
But that is because I am not old yet

There is so much time to walk from the spring Park to the garden of oddly shaped flowers

And in between I will be planting my own flowers
The forest I breathed to life
The microgreens I kissed to sleep

And the fear ebbs away as the flowers cover my eyes: I would lose the past any day
To stare at the beautiful garden of the present

The Day It Snowed in Africa

The sky fell in love with the ground
So deeply she pulled herself towards it
And cried when the earth didn't move
Did not open its arms for her embrace

She covered the trees with heavy tears
And built on the soil heaps of ice
She laden herself over every grass blade
Because she wanted the ground to feel
What she felt

Trapped in enchantment
Cold in the centre of the flame
Sick of the beauty
And heavy

She thought she was so special
Being snow in Africa
But she couldn't blame the land
Wanting what it was used to

So the snow went to Europe
Where it was welcomed coldly
And she stayed content
Finding someone who actually wanted her

Ya Lil Boat

Self-respect is the biggest paradox you might come across

It is not selfish
It is healthy
It is for the people around you
Self-respect is a privilege of being alive

Self-respect is the little boat out at sea that carries you to your next destination

And if the sea tumbles you over and wrecks the boat
You build

You own all the wood that can carry you to paradise

Wound

Time with yourself is the skin that grows beneath the scab
Prioritise it

The Pharmacy

Hello Pharmacist? Please I need your help
These days I have not felt
Two scopes of happiness in a
Caramel cone of calm
Some forgiveness on the side
With a spoon made of charm

Hey there Pharmacist
I need something stronger that lasts a bit longer
My tongue is losing its buds
I can barely taste the sorbet lime
And my hands are way too shaky
So maybe a bowl this time

Hi Pharmacist
Give me more of that raisin and rum
It once got me out of my slum
Reminds me why I come here
And a burnt waffle too please
Drowned in a mound of syrup
The supple flavour of mapled ease

Listen Pharmacist
Do you have any suggestions?
You think vanilla acceptance?
It brings out the yellow in my eyes
And you know… the usual
The stuff that numbs everything
Why not! It's my funeral

The People Who Keep You Sick

They are obsessed with their own power
If you have to beg for attention
They must leave your life

23:15 – 6th September 2022

Forgiveness is a gun
Cocked by the hands of power
But power doesn't have fingers
To pull the trigger

Forgiveness
It's the moment of submission
When you realized you have to put the gun down
Because what else is going to happen?
What can a gun heal?

Our Synaptonemal Complex

What is co-existence if all "time apart" ever is, is good for us? When we touch it is always so passionate and ravishing because maybe it's the last my hand grips with loving intentions. Someone needs to tell us our bodies are more than chequered boards. They are gorgeously-engineered sanctuaries for our hearts. However, sanctimonious they may be because the irony is: our hearts themselves are worth much less than what we think; our hearts are not solid gold otherwise our chests would sag and our ribs would break with something other than self-righteousness. Someone needs to yell at me that my heart is humble enough to hand to you for more than two seconds. My hands are soft, but they will not fracture under than weight of yours even after a lifetime. Our love is special so why do we spend our time thinking we deserve "more" when "more" is fictitious? That is like saying the world is a terrible place when you are born by the breath of the sun.

We need to pause and see that it is not about us at all. It's about Love: the lonely man on the side of the road who plays his guitar and refuses nothing but apples.
He cries for the wind that became a breeze because there was no longer pollen to play with. We have to do it for him, because some stranger stopped on the side of the road and offered this Man the most precious thing and He skipped a hundred miles, with a fistful of dehydration just so He could present us with the most exquisite gift of all time.

No, we do not love for ourselves.
How dare we be so selfish?

Everyone Needs a Little Love

My favourite things are so random
Soft blankets, ducklings
Mothers and babies, watering cans, bandages

I thought I was strange
But no, I just need the nurturing kind of love
And that's okay

Read It Again

You have to forgive yourself
Because you have to admit you fucked up

Valley

You are anfractuous like a valley, and I am smooth like liquid
We were supposed to marry the laws of nature so willows could grow alongside us
But you are a riverbed and I am mist
From the outside we were exquisite individuals
But together we were heterogeneous
I wandered through a net of trees
And you were filled with nothing, expecting streams
One of us stood empty
The other was barely present
And we called it a relationship

You can have all the love of the world
But nature will still be the heart of compatibility

Our Relationship Was Like Knitting Grass

The idea was great, artistic, exciting
But the activity made no sense
We made pretty ornaments
Not winter-weathering blankets
No matter how idealistic we began
Our whittle was inevitable

Tap Root

You've just been planted
You're no tap root, you're adventitious
One day you will be part of the grove
But for now don't confuse yourself
With my pillars, my roots
If you want me, you will grow in
The spotted sunlight underneath
The canopies of my family

You have to prove you want to stay
Because it truly is beautiful here
And I will let no weeds grow amongst the most breath-
taking trees a land can be blessed with

The Human Body

The human body is so clever
It makes you crave things when you need them
And so hunger and thirst and sleepiness are parallels to and
undeniable proof that every emotion you have is valid
If you're empty you need love
If you're lonely you need nurture
If you're anxious you need compassion
Never settle because. You. Will. Never. Have. To
Your body knows what it needs
Listen to it

Peter Parker, or Just a Parker

It's okay to forget to be kind
You are not the villain if you forget to be the hero
You're allowed to just be the journalist that works next to the red-head who was thrown out of the window
You're allowed to laugh because the invading aliens chasing after the hero look fuckin' weird
It's okay to shrug and go "fuck that's not my problem dude." Just be a bystander
A free-living peripheral
The friendly neighbourhood neither-here-nor-there
Find relief in the unspectacular
Enjoy being general cast
Steal something from set and no-one will notice except the fuckin' weird x-ray vision aliens but who gives a fuck about them
Pressure is overrated, my friend
If the world is ending, it's okay to save yourself first

Fire Escape

I will eternally be grateful for what you did for me
You did what I wasn't strong enough to do
I just wish you didn't tear down the building
You could have just taken the stairs

Dear Self

The bruises started rising as surprises, because I have never blackened like the fruit that lies still in the bowl in my kitchen

My skin complexion looks its best under denim and cotton, which works out well because the cold grips me tighter than everyone else in the room

My neck looks like it carries the weight of the world in my head, so heavy that the strings holding me together might snap if a laugh a little too authentically

Someone tell my why that dress that fit so perfectly a few months ago now sags like I am a child

Someone tell me why people stopped calling me beautiful and started calling me pretty

Someone tell me why silly little ditty me forgot to keep eating like it wasn't the paper of my leather-bound book

Because now I look at myself
A wispy little cloud
Barely anything
When I once actually cared

When I once gifted the land heavy rain
Cried down on the rivers and fed life through the valley
Filled space in the sky
Like I belonged there

And today I beg myself
Give me volume again

POEMS ABOUT PEOPLE IN COFFEE SHOPS

The Hummingbird

She is obsessed with vibrant colour
And tassels and acoustic music

She dances between chairs
Folding serviettes into birds

She concentrates too hard on one thing
But sees the entire world when she opens her eyes

Her eyes hold beautiful images
Of the skies and the ocean

Her mind turns continuously
Strolling through unorthodox libraries

Her hands touch and caress the Earth
And knead the dough to nourish her body

Her body embraces the trees
And catches the sun in the shade

She's the fondest lover,
The honest, the selfless, the sage

She's the shine of the wings of a hummingbird
The white of the moon
The sleeves of a dress
The whicker of a basket
The masterpiece and the artist

Moon and Back

I keep a lot of secrets,
I hide them between old records
Under my socks in a crowded draw
In my empty violin case
But I pack them all neatly in a box
And with my arms full I sit before you
And everytime I see you I empty that box
Because I keep no secrets from you

My deepest concerns are private
Double locked in a titanium case
Under the staircase amongst dusty clutter
An item of unremarkable discard
But every time I visit you I'll always remind you
That the first night I locked the case
Without any hesitation
I ran to you to give you the key

I don't trust anybody
Not even with a single penny I don't trust their promises
their smiles
Their intentions
But I trust you with my own life

My tears can't help but shed when I hear your words "You are going to be alright, my love."
"You are so strong, my love."
"You are right to be upset, my love."
"There is always a solution, my love."
"I love you, my love."

You saved me

Ellabella

She's fragility, age, aching, and smutty from flaky tear drops and clammy fur
She limps up the stairs and cries when you stroke her back with a heavy hand
She eats like she has never before but gains no weight at all
She breathes through a blocked nose and smells a little sour if you go too close

But her eyes are green and lively
She still sprinkles when she hears the kettle tick
She wails behind your closed door until you let her in She sits on you no matter your discomfort
And she will come back for more even though you obliviously fling her across a dark room while adjusting your blanket in the middle of the night

She is not going to live forever
She is one of my best friends
And I tell her everyday that I love her
Oh, to love someone who might never know what it means
To love someone who might never say it back
But, oh, to love…

The Elderly Man in the Airport

Orange converse
Straight jeans
Tweed jackets
Padded sleeves
Collar-crewneck combo
Semi-moon glasses
Ice blue eyes
Cotton white ponytail
Duffel bag traveller

Garden

In the garden there are hordes of mosquitoes that fly by the spool
Some powdery bugs bobbing with no direction at all
Beetles humbling along the soil and scuttling up trees

In the garden there's a dog, the sweetest golden creature
heavenly if the rest of the place were not divine
He lumbers up to a girl in a blue flannel sitting against a white wall

Pecan nuts on the ground delved deep in the soil by the bare feet of quiet and wise people
Leaves of all shades with deep dark veins reaching for the sun
Conglomerate life pumping through the arteries of the garden

And there is this most magnificent sunflower with a face the size of a frying pan
Its petals tiny slices of mango fruit
And it sags heavily
With its head hung low towards the ground
And it cries, very softly and very slowly

Until it dies

Only a few months later
Little green fingers finger their way to the surface
They pull themselves above the soil to see the light of day

They stretch for the sun like its rays are Mother's milk
And they are almost as magnificent as the one who bore them

The saddest sunflower in a place divine

And the writer wrote not of the artwork but of intricate canvas woven within

The sunflower rooted in the most nourishing of soils
With the most giving of suns on her neck

So giving and nourishing that she cried in happiness for weeks with her face towards the ground because she knew her seeds would inhabit the richest home she could give them

Even if she would not be there to see them grow

And the girl, leaning against the white wall, wiping her tears with a blue flannel, she cried

For this most selfless sunflower

The Invincible Man

He is an austere gentleman by day, and a puppy by night. He loves deeply, to the magna of this planet's core

His wisdom is rich, as is his stupidity, but he laughs at himself and carries on with the day

He will call your emotions "exaggerated" instead of "dramatic" Sometimes he can't even control his own recklessness and you have to yell in his face to get him to listen

He is not a show-horse carer, but sometimes he forgets to tell you he is still in love with you

He has a honey tongue and can write stories like a calligrapher although he puts himself through the terrible agony of reading 1800s books about war and peace and evolution

He gasps at pretty rock formations and shaves his legs once in a while
His music is the wackiest mixture you've ever heard.

He studies the human psyche of confidence and decides to be nobody you'll ever meet

He melts when baby animals are around and pretends to know how to cook, and he'll put on the most riveting performance you'll ever see upon stubbing his toe

He does the rain dance just so he can see you and he'll squeeze you just on the verge of passing out when he does

He'll play with your hair when you're feeling sick and he'll race to get an onion when you've been stung by a bee

He'll make you wooden rings and collect bricks for no apparent reason

He will cheer up the loneliest littlest person in the room, and looks at you like he has nothing to lose. Once he has chosen you, he will never let you go

He has a sly smile that will always get him where he wants to go. Emotions like guilt and self-doubt don't exist in his world

I wouldn't be surprised if he disappeared for a while and lived off the land

And soon he will start correcting you when you say he does not care about you, he'll read deep literature and sit in coffee shops just to watch the people

He will stare at you blissfully when you're touching his hair, he'll forget about his phone when you are around

He'll look forwards to long car trips and sitting silently in nature

He'll start loving all the things you love about yourself, slowly start nesting a spot in his heart for your beloved cat too

He'll take the time to cook your favourite meal, help your gran bake pastries, love your mom's dramatic stories

He'll stop treating you like you're a decoration

And soon he will become the real love of your life

The Man in a Jar

The writer
Balancing the words into a delicate sculpture using the lightest of touches, materialises a story so fragile. Words so soft to dap away the tears of the most careless stranger. He is a stock-standard broken poet

The shell
Scrambling to find pieces of himself in a forest of dry grass and shrivelled mushrooms. He hides from the truth but behind walls eroding away. And all at once he is at the mercy of the world but has a grasp on the complexities of the universe

The nomadic soul
Searching for answers in the barren miles of wasteland, he smells the sand in the air and sees tattooed into the surface etched into its skin, the lifetimes of many like him who lived when there was water, but he is so thirsty

The man in the jar
Once he gets to the ocean he dives and is swilled deep in its depth. Keep the air in your lungs, he thought, if you scream you can't float

And his body will dry in the heat of the sun. In an oasis between the desert and the ocean

Grey-green Eyes

He looks to the skies
And sees the stars in broad daylight
The stars that dotted his eyes the nights
He lay in the wild

He looks to his feet
The ones that carried him up the hill
And another and another
Until they bled red and blessed
Him with summiting the mountain

He looks to the scene around him
And sees blurs and shapes
For he shyly cries and tries to mend
His pieces, yet he doesn't know he
Is more complete than most of the world

He looks to his hands
Cleanly gripping the earth that gave him peace
And pieced him together like he belonged
Here with the ever-changing trees
Like himself, asymmetrical art

All the most beautiful things are fragile
Like the ceramic man that had seen life
Life through grey-green eyes

As the Sun Sets

Rose gold touches the earth
Pink mist flows through the wavering shadowy grasses of Africa
Orange dust settles upon the fields
Hazy purple mountains
Bruised blue sky horizon

Harry styles on the radio
A hand surfing through the wind out the car window grazing plump horses and
Parliaments of thick green trees huddled around farmhouses
Dipping hills
Hitchhiking men on dusty roads with worn out shoes

An autumn tree stretching through a half-built abandoned home
Leaves reaching through frameless windows
And branches yawning out of the roofless rooftop

A woman with golden hair
Hands ten and two
Watching the colours of the horizon opposite to the setting sun

The reason I am here
The reason I stayed

Little One

Look at the big bold world, little one

All the sights and sounds
The sun sets only for you
The heavens that open and throw colours across the sky
For the wander in your face

The ocean, the gentle touch, sneaks up unto the shores that spread out on the cold hard sand
Reaching to tickle your toes
Just to hear your laugh, little one

Look at the birds that wail for you to sing along
And the dogs so eager to greet you
The books waiting for their pages to be blessed by your bright eyes
The mirror that yearns to wear your beauty just one time

It's such a big bold world, little one
Go see it!

Waiting Room

The girl opposite me

With pink hair, split ends obscured by a hoodie
The edges of her nails stripped away
Her eyes tired and masked with monochrome make-up
Her neck is a give-away to her thinness
It's probably not the only thing she hides under
Her oversized clothes
If mental health was shown like a bruise
People would treat her like imported glass

The girl opposite me
Yet the girl exactly the same as me

Brown Eyes

Your eyes were rich brown, warm, dark chocolate, starry
when you saw the sun come up, hazy after lying in the grass
loving every time I smiled at you

Puppy when you wanted a snack, wide when you met out
new kitten, glossy with every sunset we watched at the dam,
closed peacefully when I tickled your head

Bright when I made pancakes for the two of us, dark when
you saw me crying, content when we were falling asleep
cloudy when we woke up

Rich brown, like the weight of the earth, the heart of a
mountain
So undeniably full of life with every second they saw
Until they no longer did

Peanut Butter

She's raw and nutty
So delectably smooth

She's covered in honey
And melts when she's warm

She's healthy and healing
An everyday delight

Sweet-salty synonymous
Coquettish, flirtatious

She fills the jar she's in
But keeps her own shape

Unlike anything else
Peanut Butter

Head in the Clouds

His eyes are fixated on the sky
As he ponders for minutes on end

And when he looks back on the ground
His life has lived itself without him

Spiders in Keyholes

The spiders in the keyholes
Bear witness to such a fascinating world, they watch…

The girl who dances sexily in the mirror when
The boy is grocery fetching
The girl who complains about the spicy curry
The boy who promises to start sketching
The girl who insists on praying together every night the boy
as he grabs the girl for a twirl and reprise
The girl as she makes sweet tea for the boy when
The boy looks at her with sparkly puppy eyes
The girl who has trust issues but opened her heart to the boy
who drinks too much wine on occasion
The girl who burns the celebration cake
The boy who brought home a three-legged alsation
The girl who sighed and swore never to like it
The boy who calls the girl's bluff
The girl who purposefully drops a biscuit when she makes
The boy's sweet tea (and the sugar is never enough)
The boy who cannot fix the flickering light bulb
The girl who will never enjoy
The boy's orchestral classical music
The girl who loves only the beach boys
The same girl who struggles to fall asleep and
The boy who dreams restlessly when
The girl is on the balcony in the early morning wind; the boy
who counts to ten

And then one day:

The boy, just the boy, who sagged like the dying houseplant

The boy wouldn't stop clutching a vase
The dog resting its head on his lap
The boy who didn't shower for days
And didn't notice the drip of the tap

And he just kept tossing the food
That neighbours brought to him saying
The Bolognese might help the boy's mood
But he had even stopped praying

The spiders watch mellowly as the boy's tears dried on his face
The boy's heart was wet cardboard
It's strings rings on the dartboard
Buried in one of the boxes that decorated his place

The boy's things were packed up stood in shock
Until the weight the boy carried physically had equated the weight the boy carried emotionally because then
The boy left and the home he once had was officially vacated

The spiders hoped nothing more than that
The boy had moved wherever the girl had gone disguised because someone had to fix the flickering
Lightbulb in the boy's sparkly puppy eyes

The Sexy Chair Dancer

Girls live with a sexy chair dancer in their heads
She awakens when hot water hits our bare skin
She emerges in high heels, gloves and fishnets and shows us
what broadway begs to offer
She pulls out a chair and flows like jazz music
She seduces the beat of the bass of the drum

The day I met the sexy chair dancer
She was sitting, legs crossed, sipping boiling
Blank coffee in an Italian cafe, her dark eyes
Shielded by a lavish brim hat
She left the cafe with nothing more than a red
Lipstick stain on a white cup and the waitress
Kissed her resignation the same way the same day
And left to follow the butterflies to Madagascar

The sexy chair dancer took my hand without touching my
skin and we waltzed through cobblestone streets
We went wine tasting in the wild strawberry fields
She told me her name was Chiara
And I laughed in a trance until Chiara with thin fingers
turned my chin towards her
She smirked as I stared at her left dimple
Her wildly curly black hair

"Darling, who do you think you are in love with? Who do
you think you're *supposed* to be in love with?"
The day I met the sexy chair dancer...

Queens

One school camp
Two minute noodles
Three detentions
The four of us
Five school years
Six tattoos
Seven skinny dips
Eight missed calls
Nine failed tests
Ten blackouts
Twelve piercings
Thirteen gum flavours
Fourteen caps stolen from
Fifteen jocks
Sixteen candy brands
Seventeen shots
Eighteen hours of music
Nineteen distinctions
Twenty hours on the road
Twenty one in the sky
Twenty two phone calls
Twenty three I love you
In twenty four hours
Twenty five running strides
Twenty six happy tears
One hundred weeks apart

Yet not a thing lost

What It Means to Be Human

Are you not a key characteristic of disaster?
A missile floating with tip sharper
A bull seeing the red dancer
A cathedral and you're the choir master

Are you not ceaselessly controlled by authority?
What possess your creativity?
Tethers you to whip fresh milk into cream
Sells you off as part of a machine

Are you not the stair at the bottom of a mountain?
A racehorse waiting for the count in
The lover of the one who shouts and
The glass at the edge of the counter

Are you not the energy that refuses to be destroyed? The
parachute shivering to deploy
The gas in a lighter nul en void
The puzzles of Sigmund Freud

The power you contain
Is the metal that reframes?
The painting of human mind

How can we be sour?
When we can use our power
To choose everyday to be kind

What it means to be human

Is to gather with our crew and
Find the beauties beneath the sea

What it means to be being
Is to see all we are seeing
And choose everyday to be free

POEMS ABOUT LOVELY THINGS

All While John Hughes Takes Notes

He dreamt of a green lake and a small breeze
Sweet smiles and slight lips
Just him and her

He tucks the hair gently behind her ear
His hands don't shake much —
Not even a little

She looks into his eyes, smiles, steps closer
Cooing water fowls
He takes his hand in hers

Alas he wakes up in a cold empty bed
Numb of a dream he
So wished would happen

And he tells her his dream sheepishly
While touching her hair
The very next day

As they stand near a green lake, a small breeze
Geese and shining water

And it turns out that they are not as invincible as they were
when they dreamt, his hands did shake a little

I Love Him So Much It Scares Me

I see you talking, your mouth moving and sometimes the words just don't run but instead float through my head and I'm distracted…

I see your illustrious hair moving by your hand and how it folds onto itself shining like Damascus metal and I'm entranced…

I can only guess what life I led before this, one divine, to have not just someone like you but you in my arms and I'm broken…

Like a grain of sugar cracked and dissolved into warm water

You have broken me in the most beautiful way possible because when I lay here before you, every millionth of me exposed

You kiss me

You kiss me with the slimmest needle, stitching me back together

Will Do Me Wonders

A hot bath with soft skin and candles
Mid-laugh surrounded by people who love me being there
An early morning wake up next to someone beautiful
A hammock and a nap in the wild
A stroll around some trees and watching strangers
A challenging game of chess

Being content

It all would just do me wonders

My Brother

Come back to hear me fall down the stairs at the sound of George Lucas's greatest creation, to laugh when you see me swoon at young Mark Hamill

Come back to give me a hug, and put your chin on the top of my head because I'm so small, tease me about being a child even though you're a little scared of me

Come back to ruffle my hair after I mastered the messy bun, and to criticise my cooking in the nicest way possible

Come back to recite all your favourite movie lines in the funniest renditions, to greet me as Captain Jack Sparrow, Jim Carrey, Shaggy whoever you want, as long as it's actually you

Come back to refuse all fast food takeaway and dessert we buy you, and sigh when we try tell you it's healthy because it makes you happy

Come back to get frustrated with my lack of punctuality Give me lecture on the smallest things and to tell me you value your life too much to witness my control a vehicle

Come back to eat every one of the blueberry muffins in the house, and drive us all nuts because you stuff the wrappers down the hollows of the couch

Come back to be the dog's favourite even though you don't

any of the dog chores

Come back for long road trips singing U2 and Johnny Clegg and having honest conversations about how we are the best pair out there no doubt

Come back to give me advice even though I don't ask for it, to be my strictest parent

Came back to find my crying and don't leave until I calm down

Come back to hold me and whisper "Ohana means family and family means forever" in your best stitch voice and hold me harder when I burst out laughing

Come back to see my fragilities and cracks, take a cold cloth to my head and wipe away the blood and glitter from my cuts

Come back to remind me that I am so strong because our hearts are made of the same untearable fabric

Come back please
Come back always

Bitter Tastes

Twisting lemons off trees
Dewey water bouncing onto your chilled bare skin

Smooth red cork-aged wine
And the bitter swirling of the brain to follow

Tea leaves that leave your mouth dry
The warm trickling down your throat afterwards

Sour flowers
In cloudy water and soft stem ends

The bone cold fire
While a kindling shallowly breaths

Halved strawberries
Glossy pink and not quite ripe just yet

Euphoric bitter tastes

The Bush Baby

Slight little thing
With orb-like marble eyes
Looking back and forth, back and forth
A whip like tail sailing behind it
As it leaps into the air and hits the tree, sticking with such posed grace
Its satellite-dish ears hearing everything around it...
The longing guttural cry of the bedraggled hyena who lost its pack the night before
The crickets shivering lyrically under the cold winter soil
The soft crunching of sand as it waves around the feet of an elephant
The violent ripping of shrubs and the fracturing of tree skeletons to follow
And the eerie whisperings from the grass floating into the smoky night sky

Sweet-sounding patterned music serenading the full moon and its choir of stars
The bubble-boiling of the sherry in a ceramic mug dug snugly into dying coals
And eventually the chittering of the excited ape-like things all pointing in her direction

She clings onto the tree
Scuttling onwards and upwards
For a closer look in a safer location at these things she has spotted...

That wear colourful skins
With hollow stringed instruments and sweet warm drinks
Who live for just a small piece of her life here in the wild

My, my wouldn't it be strange to live like one of them

Love, a Place

Laying on our backs on the hard floor, listening to Busyhead on repeat, whispering the words that we can't relate to and don't understand but we still feel

Climbing through small window frames to sit on the roof risking it all for the stars that we weren't paying much attention to

Walking hushly through grassy plains guided by nothing but the bright moon, the only parts of our bodies warm are our hands intertwined

Baking pancakes when the whole neighbourhood is asleep and dreaming, just not as lustrously as we are

Sharing a bottle of whiskey and playing chess by candle light soft blankets and sleepy eyelids, falling in love with falling in love

21:26 – 20th July 2022 – Today Was a Beautiful Day

The early morning sun reddens the far distance
An ominous fire, blackening the trees on the horizon
And sucking up the rivers of mist that blanket the sleeping water

The morning sun hits the trees with gold
Ripening the green leaves like autumn apples
The earthly saturater, breathing life into the savanna

The mid-morning sun fringes the wavering grasses silver
Tickling the ground with something warm
And the copper fizz settles between the stalks

The lunchtime sun cracks the top of the sand on the dirt roads
And spills shadows onto the ground like sheets lain out
For the acacia trees as the sun rocks them to sleep

The afternoon sun dips in the sky
Blinding half of the world until it melts into the cloud bank
And ducks down into the velvety darkness

The late afternoon sun is hidden but stubborn
Gripping the earth in gaps it finds between the clouds
Crying for its own rest, weeping from the separation to the world

The evening sun is sacrificed for the rain

The clouds bellow over, wetting the earth beneath
The giant in the sky moves his heavy armchair to watch

The sun accepts rest, the orange eye slowly closes for the evening, batting its sleepy eyelashes until the stars dance upon its eyelids

No sunset today but rather
The smell of wet plants and settled dust
Today was a beautiful day

06:21 – 24th July 2022 – Sounds

The *begaggling* of the noisy birds
The *pewt-pewt* of the hiding owlet
The scutter-scurrying of the grassy creatures
The *wa-wa-wa-walligogging* of the Egyptian goose
The *croop-croop* of the bush thrushes

The *umbarku* bark of the alarmed chacma baboon
The shrieking of the birds to follow
The *flip-flap-flip* of bird wings slapping together
The cough of the impala as it leaps over the grasslands The hurried thudding of hooves against hard sand
And then quiet

The light lapping as the cat going for her morning drink

One of My Happiest Moments

Sticky mornings with unbrushed hair
Bright eyes and warm smells
Nestled into our clothes
Socks and thrown-together outfits
As we shuffle into the bakery
And pick out some chocolate croissants
Some fresh orange juice
To totter back home with
And then I can answer the longing call
From the bed within your arms

A Cute One

You must be a catch because
I can't stop fishing for compliments

01:47 – 26ᵗʰ August 2022

There is something so chivalrous about this light
It doesn't just take my hand but it holds it
It whispers foreign languages against my neck
It wraps around me like no other material
The light fills the room but not selfishly but as if
It does so to see my eyelashes wave against one another
To watch as I braid my hair, sip my tea, read
It shines to see the edges and curves of my face
To make a metaphor tangible and coat me in gold
Oh, kind light, hug yourself around me again
Love me beautiful
Until the world dare parts two such pieced-together souls

Doll

You spend your days with a pair of scissors
Fastened neatly in your gentle hands
Snipping away at my insecurities and revealing
My prettiest things, dusting away the split ends
That fall slowly on my arms and sweeping them
Away with other dirt like it's so easy to make
Another individual feel so complete just like that

Breast

Her body is the sunrise to a blind man
Her anatomy soft peaches
Her smoothness like shells from the river
Her voice breaks the land from the sea

When you hear the word "woman"
Does your breath shiver like it should?
Because woman is the core of the Earth
Woman is what warms the sun
Woman is every piece of life that
Inhabits this planet because without
Woman there is no heart
No food
No shelter
For no youth

Every time a woman's body is humiliated
The plates that hold life shudder in disgust

For the earth quakes when the woman breaks
Woman is the backbone of life itself

Wilderness

The smell of the cold
Frost etching into your cheeks
As you brave the wind and its swaddling arms
The sky as it burns
Red on the horizon and black everywhere else
Speckled with twinkling eyes
And the blinking glimpses on the ground
Of the never-sleeping bugs on the floor of the wild
Dry trees reaching towards the sky
Into the smokey grey mist smudged on the canvas
The sand crunches and the wild stops to listen

Hush

You feel your blood run hot and your skin crawl cold
As the red burns away like the dying kindles of an embering fire
You feel this weird sensation that makes you shiver
Like you can hear the breathing of the trees that surround you
The flicker at the corner of your mouth that brings life into your frozen face
And you feel it
In your bones

Elation

Butterfly Photography

Love is like butterfly photography

Some people get lucky and some people don't. To capture the little fluffy insect dipping and bobbing between the green shoots. To charm the graceful creature while it sniffs the damp earth and it surfs in the breeze is nothing to do with holding the art but rather experiencing the art. You wait for this butterfly to nestle on the dandelion right in front of you and hold your breath because in a breath it could quaver away and leave you alone. Until one day you are granted the most beautiful reality and hold this soft insect, a lifelong youthful butterfly and a few blank photos of pretty vegetation.

It doesn't happen to everybody
Patience is required
Love is like butterfly photography

Sleep, My Lover

Seeing yellow birds flutter between lichen-coated branches with a cold grey drizzly sky as the background is my favourite thing. Because it means I can be like those I am so jealous of: the trees covered in blankets with a license to do nothing, to move nowhere, no responsibilities except to stand and happily sigh as life weaves around them. I can delve a little deeper into the warm softness of my bed and close my eyes and listen to nothing but chirps and wallows and calls and whistles. Until I dazedly crawl into the comforting arms of sleep, my lover, as I dream I am a yellow bird flying free with the rest of the pretty wild things

My Sympathy to the Light Sleepers as the Deep Sleeping Insomniac

We are often awake at the same time
In the coldest hours of the morning
In a state between sleep and wake
You'll find us dwelling in the same listless zone

Maybe sometimes we could drink tea together
Slice an orange you picked in the garden
Imagine we could be companions in the lonely hour and
share the last slice of cake in the hungry hour

Your brushstroke creases and my dull half-moons
Could frame the same smiling eyes
We could both forget about our responsibilities
And listen until the thunder becomes a biscuit crumble

Rachel

I am obsessed with you because you offer me candid photography, a better self-esteem and adventure

Detangling My Flaws

On days like this I need to nurse my weak
And treat myself gently
Letting the brush flow through the knots
Massaging my roots in oil
Letting the conditioner sink in
The warm water rinse away the dirt
Letting the air undress the curls
A field of hazel silk and satin
I let my fingers surf their lightness
On days like these I braid my flaws
Into intricate weaves and waterfalls
Secure some pins for stability
What a wonder to just ... be

The Maiden Envy

Lovers sweet touch of the first time
Careful passion and stifled gasps
Because this won't be the last time we stow
Away and hide amongst each other's bodies

I want to see your face curl for the first time
And your hands find their grips on my body
Your fingers through my hair
Like they are looking for wheaten fronds

We will never know what it was like
To discover what that tingle means
Unfolding each other's pleasures

We will never find ourselves
While losing such promiscuities
I will never know the meaning of Shakespeare chanting from
your lips on lover's silks

I will never be praised for my youthfulness
And my skin soft like milk my hair tumbling
Along your naked body that which is subject to art

I will never find homage in your arms like you
Offer only baby animals in the cold of night
In the barns of the farm you work on

My face your cup, my body yours to uncover
We won't picnic the things you steal from the kitchen

And feel the wind on our naked backs

Make me a maiden because I want you
To define love for me
I am envious that I know the logistics of sex
Before I found out what making love was all about

That Jacaranda Love

It was a sudden burst of lilac from a dull unimportant tree
Immediate vibrance causing chaos in its dwindling temperamentality
They always look dispensable, armfuls of flowers falling at your knees
Knitting purple blankets that aren't used to bare the breeze
And soon when the tree is naked, brown, barren and keeled
You won't have a daily reminder why you fell head over heels
Besides the once-off courteous dove
Paint me when I am a winter jacaranda and I will know it's real love

The Feeling Falling for Love

Eloquence
Smooth like marble
A candle's steady burn

Mountains at blue dusk
The dark ocean underwater
On a wave less night
Glow in the dark graffiti
Slow waltzing jellyfish

Murmuring to the stars
Our childish dreams
Heavy blankets on tired bodies
The dim am light sifting
Through like powdered sugar

The piano melodies
And meadows of lavender
On the bare backs of
Galloping horses
The hold of lifting wind

Rose gold clouds
Far away thunder
Midnight ice cream

Play That Elevator Music, White Boy

A relationship is like sharing a flute of champagne to celebrate our effervescent souls
Dancing with a curtain between our bodies
It is directing an 80s comedy TV shows while blindfolded and playing arcade games after a few cosmopolitans

Relationships are magnets, push and pull
We spend our time catching the equilibrium point, except I am catching waves and you are catching fly fish. When one is falling out of love the other would give them a reason to wander back like a limping puppy

I've been a participant in this toxic tango for too long now when the human tongue tastes something salty, it always craves something sweet and that is how our relationship became a contradiction. That is how we played chess on a dartboard and crafted a pretty little umbrella of lace

Darling, I simply can do this no longer, we are going to waltz lessons next Monday morning

Dutch Apple Pie

Today I am healing
Sinking into soft delicacies of my duvet
Letting the pillows cloud my judgement
And snoozing until the strength sets in

Today I am healing
The gentle breeze on the back of my neck and the
Warmth of my belly as I curl into
A little rose of blankets like a field mouse

Today I am healing
I have not breathed responsibility-less air
In a while and it is so refreshing I wish to do so
With eyelids quietly shut

Today I am healing
Feeling like a little warm Dutch apple pie
In the oven that bakes happy and healthy
Reminding myself of my sweetness

Today I am healing
Photosynthesising in my autogenic hope
Fallowing in the clean, the love, the soft
Sighing in the haze of self-reconciliation

Today I am breathing

POEMS THAT ARE PRETTY TRUTHS

Foundations

All I do is for the people I love
The music I listen to is so I can share it with them on long car trips
The food I eat is to keep them happy and healthy
The photos I take are to decorate the walls of their homes
The path I tread is so they can embrace me with pride in the end
I pretend to love myself so I can fit in with my favourite people
Until I stumbled into a small hole in my own heart
And I became something that made it beat stronger
And I actually quite liked feeling so substantial
It was like I could build a home for my loved ones to stay
And their livelihoods flourished so much that it made me think
That maybe there is something worth loving here

23:34 – 7th March 2022

Toppled cloth piles and tossed wash baskets later, you're digging into your old boxes in the attic...
So dusty your lungs clean the air around you
Deep down somewhere amongst the war-sawn varsity-room band flags
 The bicycle pumps that are always so useful until you have to use them—
Amongst the symbolic leashes of your favourite dog companion
The besmattered shirt from when you ran around playing paintball with your childhood friends
That pair of shoes you never had the heart to say goodbye to because you love telling everyone that one of the laces is actually a tent string from a school camping trip

Amongst a hoarder's delight of a life well documented with rubble and boxes—
You search through your most good-for-nothing-but-a-reason-for-daylightless-storage-gems-something-to-fill-the-space, concealed treasures of nostalgia in the visibility of your hallway...

And then you pull out the one thing
You've missed the most
Your fingertip touches its sharp edges
And your old sweatshirt undoes
The dust that covers the view
Of what you've so wished
To find for such a long time...

You see them reflected back in the glass

They look tired
Aged like cheese forgotten
There is mould underneath their eyes
And cracks and scars across their forehead

Their neck skin sags like
They've been pulled in every direction
And their hair is shredded at the ends
And dying at the roots

Where had they been for so long...

You have never been so relieved
To recognise someone in your entire existence:
Your entire existence

And they are beautiful
And you forgot them for a while
But now you remembered who they were
How they laughed how they loved
How they felt to be in their skin
And all over again you fell in love with yourself - holding a dirty mirror in an immaculate hallway

Missing them so terribly, you engulf them into a hug and all they say is:

"I missed you too."

11:12 – 11th May 2022

I woke up this morning with a spark inside
An excitement to travel through the bush
A smile brought on by my favourite songs
A hunger

A want to put confused smiles onto strangers' faces
A yearning to be held by someone I loved
A longing to kiss
An appreciation for the light streaming through my blinds
A feeling a warmth when I lie my hand in the sun
A blissful heavenly feeling

Most of all I felt a relief
Relief washing through my whole body
Cold and clean
Like the heavily-choked laugh after submerging under an ice-cold waterfall
The enigmatic feeling of letting go

Because sometimes I thought I'd never feel this way again
When actually it was waiting to embrace me the whole time

You Fell in Love With Me Through a Window

As I draw my curtains apart
Standing on a dusty chair hanging bands flags
On once plain unremarkable walls
And stringing photos of palm trees and beaches across the room
I almost pull down the curtains tying the string down to the curtain hook
Wearing bright pink tie-dyed pants

You fell in love with the way I listened to Bon Jovi
How I danced when the pina colada song came on
And the sweet quiet words I used to sing with Billie
The face I pulled when my microwave almost fell off the counter

You walked past my room and always stopped to stare you'd hear me play the guitar
The same boring chords over and other until it sounded like something
The orange light illuminating my window
My messy loose hair
And the oversized shirts I wore
How I talked with people on the phone for hours
The dirty jokes I told my friends
How I spoke to my mom about everything

The tone in my voice when I said "I love you"
Emphatically, repeatedly

You fell in love with how easily my kitty-cats-in-cups
Socks would immediately brighten my mood
And how I cacconed myself in a fluffy blanket when I was sad
The scarves in my hair, the books on my shelf
The photos I chose to take
How I would stare at the sunset and the stars and the clouds the way you stared at me

I fell in love with you through a window

My Home

My girl is easily distracted
She's always watching strangers
Observing people from a distance
Not many look back
But some do
Captivated by her mystic
Just like myself

And she follows their eyes, staring back
Looking away
From an outsider's perspective
She acts coy
And even I look at her
I look at myself
And there is this sinking feeling

I wonder why she would do that
Look at strangers
As if I wasn't sitting next to her
And I squeezed her hand
With furrowed eyebrows
Questioning

And she just smiles timidly and says
"They are beautiful."
And my heart breaks a little
She sees it in my eyes and cocks her head
Inching ever so closer and whispers

"But they aren't home…"
She wraps her arms around me like she will never let go
"You are home."

Fungalore

Mining for gold is the cruellest thing
Hacking away and encased in the babble
Of his fellow miners speaking mixed dialects
He lost touch with open air and civilization

Chugging down an unstable tract
Excited at the slightest glimmer
And realises it's his own heavy cold tools
That tricked his heavy cold eyes

Eyes that blinked too many times
That shy away from the sunlight
That are no strangers to dirt and sweat

Hit. Drag
Lift. Hit.
Drag. Lift
Hit. Hit. Hit. Hit.

No clunk of gold
But tears, sobbing
Gasping for air
The miner is on his knees

Humbled to the core of the earth
By the core of the earth
That which he wasn't far from
Cursing his own oblivion

The first time his eyes met gold
Was the first time his gloves of dirt come off his hands

Because You Asked

"Are you warm enough?"
Simply one of the most caring sentences ever spoken

I Swam through the Salty Water for more Salty Water

You really do have an indescribable love for
The dawn when you thought you might die in the night for
the sand when you almost drowned in the ocean

Makes you want to cry really

What Is a Kind Heart?

The perfect field is when the grass just touches the tips of my fingers as I walk
And the ground sucks up all the sounds of laughter a play it back like background music
I can run barefoot and not worry about the stones, and can be naked and not worry about the bugs
There is nothing between me and the earth, the lightning can touch me and still be grounded
The acacia trees will have thorns made of honey and the sun won't be so harsh because the sky is such a striking shade of azure blue
The soil can absorb all the goodness of the world and the sugar will osmote through the soles of my feet and
Move into my xylem and pull through my body; and this is my medication
The clouds will pass above abundantly; like paint that was left over on the palette and everything will be textured and tasteful
It is the least lonely place on the planet and it feels right to spend this time with myself
This is something I have rarely experienced
This is peace

Having a kind heart is walking through this land with arms full of empty glass jars
Bending down and scooping up a handful of soil, a fistful of fronds and a few chunks of acacia bark and stuffing the jar
Having a kind heart means carefully taking these jars home and leaving them in the sunlight and allowing the contents to

ferment like a sourdough starter
Having a kind heart is a pantry is brimming, a jar for everyone who is hungry
Having a kind heart is kissing this feeling onto the lips of those who forgot how wonderful it was to taste the raw batter of the world

Impala Lily

There are many watering cans for the impala lily in the left hand side of my chest
There is a small little blue one with baby pink flowers that offers water sweet from the mountains
There is a large one, royal purple, plump and vivacious, filled with clouds
There is a timid one, thin and beige, filled with the water that was used to rinse the coffee beans
A white one with turquoise swirls brimming with mint-ginger tea
And finally the clumsy water jug

But I was never the best at measuring
My plant thirsted for too much of the water from the jug
I asked you for a lake to keep me alive in hopes of getting a few drops
I am only a tweed because you accidentally split

And I convinced myself that you weren't starving me you were teaching me that I needed to be hated so I could grow taller
That I was a plant that looked pretty while choking

So that is why I lost so much weight
Why my leaves dried up and crumbled
Why I didn't recognise myself in the end

For a water jug who didn't know my worth

How can I not be grateful that you poured onto the floor instead of into me?
How can I not be grateful that you forced me to learn how to survive?
How can I not be grateful that you taught me to see the colour of my world? Those begging to give me water? The ones who love me?

Because, now, watch me thrive

12:17 – 26th September – Rising

That feeling, she came back
Your pen was touching paper
And suddenly the world was
Touching you in the same way
Scribbling all over you, inscribing
Weakness delicately into your bones
The heavy blinking tires you out
And lowers the frequency of
Your surroundings like you are in
The belly of a vibrating radio
The lump in your throat beats
Aggressively against the walls
Of your skin, a thousand prisoners
Are trapped somewhere inside
They want out and you want in
You want in on your own mind
The twiks of the electricity
That spark every muscle of your
Body and the collars that hold
The thoughts inside that have
Slipped off to let the dogs run
Ballistic through the fields…
The fields, the beautiful fields
The many fields where every piece
Of you resides, the fields
Of wheat that feed your spirit
The fields of tulips that
Nurture you back to yourself
The fields… the fields you breathe

Flower pheromones into your
Coagulant lungs burnt by the
Water... the water you inhaled when you
 Left the land to fend off the beasts
Of the sea, the heart of the
Tidal waves, the waves that
Surfaced you just for long enough
So you wouldn't fall through the
Water the way the first blossom
Dies ... dies and sinks ... and sinks
Off the arms of the green lovers of sweet buttery-scented alyssum
Plooms in the fields, the gorgeous
fields... the fields you breathe
The breath of the berries on the
Bushes around you, the soil
Beneath your nails as you dug
The soil which gave birth to daisies
Dancing dolefully like brides
On your fingertips, freedom
Tastes so sweet because the
Oxygen from the flowers
Around you reach into your body
And massage your heart back
Into beating the right rhythm
And your first step out of the
Womb of the field follows
The drum of the song of the
World calling your name
She almost controlled you but
She forgot that it was your
fingers that gripped the pen

A Letter to Who I Want to Be

I am the one who turns heads in library isles
My face you've sworn you've seen before

I want your breath to falter when I brush you
And you just don't know what it is about me
That makes you so childishly appealed to the stripped
Anklet and the oversized Vans, the loose jeans and the
Wavy hair, the naked face and the idiosyncrasies
I want to whip milk into cream into butter for you
And make your coffee better than you've ever liked it
I want you to fall in love with everything that is right
With the world by seeing it in the reflection of my eyes
I want you to breathe in everything we take for granted
That feeling of speed at night, trees that litter petals,
Blind men singing, elderly lovers locking gaze
I want you to see the flowers in my hair that find and deliver
the pretty things to the open doors of my mind
Into rooms decorated with words strung together like pearls
from an ancient shipwreck
I want you to teach yourself to flirt, trying to catch my smile
Sneak it into a bottle and replay it when you can't sleep
I want to be the flower that turned on horticulture for the
rocketeer

I wanted to be so extraordinary that I made your arms heavy
with the thought of me wrapped in them

I wanted want
And I got it, overwhelming amounts

If feathers were compliments I would have I would have a room of pillows
Yet I would still lay awake at night

I wanted a want so gripping it made me feel like it was worth all the years of being alone
And I had only heard of one individual who's smile
Could supposedly make you feel irreplaceable

And here I am wanting no want more than hers
Her attention, her compassion, her kindness
I fell in love so deeply with her

The one who decided to love herself but not by
Beating it into herself like she tried to for years
The one who cleaned every piece of floor my feet touched
The one for feed me richly like I was a temple of God

No longer do I want to be the desired
The gem, the intelligent
The extraordinary
To everybody else

All I want is to be the one who wants herself first

Coming Down

One day you just wake up
You walk upstairs
Look in the mirror
Splash some water on your face
You continue climbing to the middle of the sky
And see the world below
Yourself amongst the images
Like you were actually a character
And now you see the premier
You reach the place you ran to
You stood in on the mountain you climbed
You built the walls of your home
And now you look down
That's you down there
How could you forget that
You were actually alive?

And you're like: "Holy smokes."
My feet are actually touching the ground now
My lungs are taking in air in this very moment
I am a walking talking dumb-founded miracle

22:04 – 1st October – Breathing Is My Favourite Emotion

Anxiety is like have eerie music playing at the bottom of your ears
Your whole day you're anticipating something bad to happen
Anxiety is your soul running away and your body standing still
Like no two senses can function at one time because it's just the wrong side of overwhelming
You can hear your brain mechanisms overheating and jamming
And you're covered in insulation tape
Anxiety is like you are trying to board a train but it doesn't stop for you to step on
It's the constant movement of your surroundings and your stasis
Like you were folded inside out and thrown into a washing machine

But when you come out you'll feel so clean and new
Like you've slept a thousand years covered in softest material you can imagine
You've hibernated in a glass of honey until the colour started refracting again

You travelled to a different place and loved it there

And it will be wonderful

I Get it from My Grandmother

My heart is soft dough, I get it from my grandmother
She taught that my softness was virtuous
That I needed nurture, warmth and time to rise
She kneaded me like my heart was the batter of bread
She taught me to treat people kindly and gently like this
But accidentally made me pliable

You can pull me apart and stretch me on a cold surface
mould me, however, you feel beautiful
Watch how I collapse at your touch, melt into you like butter
How I clutch and cling to your warm fingers
And make yielding strings out of myself when you manipulate me

My first mistake was believing the world would know how soft I was and was meant to be

My first mistake was thinking the world would know a good thing

Yet my gentleness I have had to hold onto
Like a child and their teddy bear
And it has been one of my greatest honours

Publishing a Book

Much like the making of a book
You must love yourself

Cover
How nature loves your face turned towards her sun
And the strangers who know nothing about you
Yet some dare to think that given a little time
You could be very important to them

Paper
The tea-bag holding flavours your loved ones make for you
The way their arms fit your body
The love indented onto the canvas of the ones who paint
You sitting on the veranda
Just to show the world the smile
On your face when you're home

Ink
How both flaws and miracles make the art inside
The type of love similar to what God holds
Unconditional with everything exposed
And trust me darling it exists more than science
Like the sun wrapped around the Earth

A Poem About Solitude

Hiking up mountains
Touching sunrises
Spending time with the clouds
Following the water

You find the gems of the world hidden where the birds sleep
Ask the monks
Or the farmers on subsistent land
The woman alone on a Greek island
Looking after her childhood home
Just as her father asked her to
The wild ones and
Wildly knowing

Alone is only so scary because it is the most powerful place to be